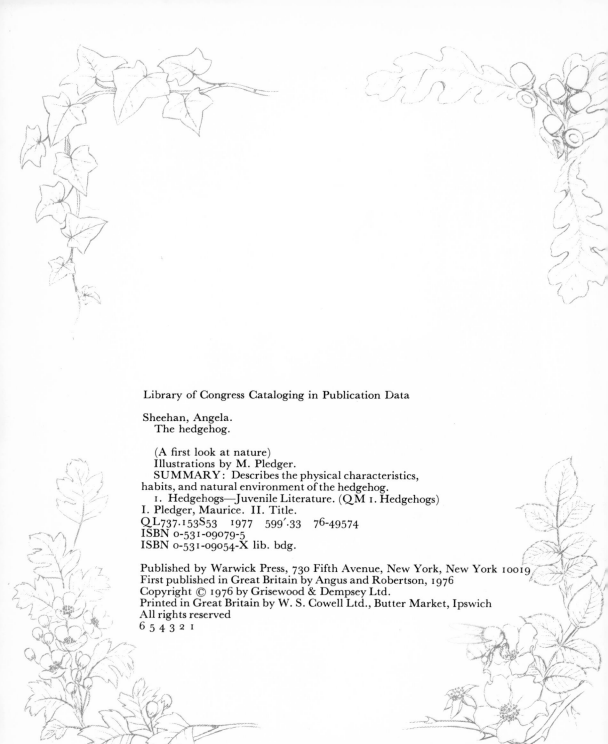

Library of Congress Cataloging in Publication Data

Sheehan, Angela.
  The hedgehog.

  (A first look at nature)
  Illustrations by M. Pledger.
  SUMMARY: Describes the physical characteristics,
habits, and natural environment of the hedgehog.
  1. Hedgehogs—Juvenile Literature. (QM 1. Hedgehogs)
I. Pledger, Maurice. II. Title.
QL737.153S53   1977   599′.33   76-49574
ISBN 0-531-09079-5
ISBN 0-531-09054-X lib. bdg.

Published by Warwick Press, 730 Fifth Avenue, New York, New York 10019
First published in Great Britain by Angus and Robertson, 1976
Copyright © 1976 by Grisewood & Dempsey Ltd.
Printed in Great Britain by W. S. Cowell Ltd., Butter Market, Ipswich
6 5 4 3 2 1

The Hedgehog

By Angela Sheehan
Illustrated by Maurice Pledger

WARWICK PRESS · NEW YORK

For three months the hedgehog had slept in a warm, snug nest under the ground. Now it was warmer, and she woke from her long sleep.

First she wanted to see if the winter had really gone. Pushing her way up through the soil, she found that the sun was shining. And there were many other animals about.

The hedgehog could smell the spring flowers and leaves. She knew that among them there would be worms, snails, insects, and many other good things to eat. As soon as it was dark she would go out to find some food.

After such a long sleep the hedgehog felt weak and very hungry. She did not really care what she ate. Sometimes in summer, she went to the farm and drank milk from the cows' udders. But it was too far to go to the farm now.

Instead, the hedgehog looked for food in the grass. She found a slug and a spider. Then she found a newt. Quickly, she stuck spines into it and bit hungrily into its tasty flesh.

As she ate, the hedgehog had to watch out that no foxes or badgers crept up on her. They were the only animals that she really feared. Their strong claws and teeth could break through the spines and kill a hedgehog, even if she rolled up into a ball.

But no enemies attacked the hedgehog that night. By morning she wasn't hungry, but she was very tired. So she hid under a pile of leaves and slept for the day.

For the first few days after she woke up, the hedgehog felt tired almost all the time. But soon she grew stronger. She liked looking for food each night. Sometimes she caught frogs by the stream.

One night, as the hedgehog made her way to the stream, she heard a noise behind her. She stopped at once and found that there was another hedgehog following her. It was a male and he wanted to mate with her.

The female took no notice of him and went on her way. But the male hedgehog ran faster. As he came close, she turned and hissed at him to make him go away.

But he did not go away. Instead, he hissed back and ran round her. Now she stood very still. Snorting and grunting, the male ran round and round her for almost three hours. As he came closer and closer, she grew less afraid of him. And in the end, she let him mate with her.

After they had mated, the male
hedgehog went off to look for food. He
found a skylark's nest full of eggs. In
seconds, all the shells were broken. The
hedgehog greedily sucked up the yolks.
There was nothing the mother bird could
do but fly away.

But the skylark was not the only animal
that saw the hedgehog attack the nest. A
fox saw him, too. And the fox was always
hungry. As soon as the hedgehog smelled
the fox, he began to run. But the fox ran,
too. The hedgehog knew that he could not
get away.

Quickly, he rolled up into a ball. The fox would find it hard to eat him now. But the fox did not give up. He sniffed at the tightly rolled hedgehog. Then he pushed it with his paw. The spiny ball began to move. The fox hit it again. This time, it started to roll. Over and over it rolled, downhill toward the stream.

Suddenly, the hedgehog was in the water. Unrolling himself, he started to swim. But then the fox pounced. His fangs sank into the hedgehog's stomach. No spines could save him now.

Hedgehogs do not live together when they have mated, as some other animals do. So the female never knew how her mate died. She went on hunting for food each night and sleeping each day. And all the time, four young hedgegogs were growing inside her.

After about a month, the hedgehog looked for a place where she could raise her young. She found a hole at the bottom of a stone wall and filled it with a soft bed of leaves. Safe inside, she waited for the babies to be born.

At first the babies were blind and deaf.
And the spines on their backs were soft
and white. But, in about two days, hard
brown spines had grown. The mother fed
the babies on milk from her body.

Sometimes when they were asleep, she
went out to find food for herself. Once,
while she was away, the young hedgehogs
crawled out of the nest to take their first
look at the world. Their mother found
them when she came home. She knew it
was not safe for them to be outside. So,
one by one, she carried them back inside
by the scruffs of their necks.

As soon as the babies could roll up to protect themselves, their mother took them out to find their own food. With so many new things to eat, they drank less milk now.

One night the whole family had a wonderful feast. The mother hedgehog found a snake. It was long, thin, and poisonous.

The young hedgehogs watched as their mother rushed round and round the snake. The snake tried to strike her with its fangs. But, instead of killing her, it got caught up in her spines.

Quickly, the hedgehog rolled up and held the snake in her mouth. The snake tried to get away but it was hurt too badly. In the end, it fell back, dead.

Eating the snake had been good fun for the young hedgehogs. But, now, as they went home, they could hardly keep their eyes open. When they reached the nest, they fell asleep in one large heap.

But the fox was not sleepy. And he had not had much to eat. Quietly, he followed the hedgehogs home. He sniffed at the bottom of the wall, but could find no way into the nest. Then he pawed at the stones until, at last, one came loose.

Now the fox could almost see the
hedgehogs. He could certainly smell them.
The mother hedgehog was still awake. She
could feel the fox's breath and hear him
panting. For a moment she faced him
bravely. But then she rolled up to be even
safer.

The young hedgehogs woke up just as
the fox pressed his nose through the hole.
They tried to back away from the
terrifying red face. Their spines stood on
end as the great animal tried to break
down the wall. But he could not get into the
nest. In the end, he went away – still
hungry.

As soon as the sun went down, the mother led the young ones from the nest. She had to find a safer place to hide them. The whole family ran silently through the wood. Before long, they found a tree with big roots under which they could live.

The young hedgehogs were soon so big that they did not really need to stay in a nest. Each night, they went farther from their mother. Soon only one of them came back to the nest in the mornings. And after a few days, the mother drove him away. He too must learn to look after himself.

The mother hedgehog almost never saw her young now. But one morning, she saw something that made her spines stand on end. A young badger had caught one of her hedgehogs and was playing with him like a ball.

But she could not help him now. With luck, the young badger had already eaten enough. Maybe it would just enjoy its game and forget the tasty meat beneath the spines.

Soon the summer was over. Cold winds blew, and berries, leaves, and nuts lay on the ground. Now all the young animals had grown up and left their parents.

Day by day, the woods became quieter. The buzz of insects stopped and the birds no longer sang in the mornings.

As the weather grew colder, all the animals began to eat more. They needed lots of fat on their bodies to keep out the winter cold.

The hedgehog ate whatever she could find. She often went out during the day now as well as at night. She knew that she would have nothing at all to eat in the winter.

Often the farmer's children left saucers of milk outside for the hedgehogs. The children knew that hedgehogs love milk. And they knew that their father did not like them stealing it from his cows. So every evening, the hedgehog went to the farm to find the milk.

The hedgehog grew fatter and fatter. But she felt tired. She did not even feel strong enough to go out and eat.

The ground would soon be hard, and the nights were long and cold. The time had come to build her winter nest.

One night she found a good place for her nest. At the bottom of an old oak tree, there was a big, thick fungus. Underneath it, the ground was dry and covered with leaves.

The hedgehog pushed the leaves into a pile. Then she dug into the soil below with her sharp claws.

When the hole was big enough, she pushed the leaves into it. She stood in the hole and turned round and round, pressing the leaves against the sides. Then she pulled the last leaves and soil down over her, and rolled into a tight ball. She could sleep safely until spring.

More About Hedgehogs

A hedgehog's head

Spines and Senses

The hedgehog is about 10 inches long. It has a fat body and short legs. Its tail is so small that you cannot see it. Its back is covered with short, sharp spines. Its head, belly, and legs are covered with hair. The hedgehog cannot see very well, but it has good ears and a sharp sense of smell.

What do Hedgehogs Eat ?

Hedgehogs can eat almost anything with their strong jaws and sharp teeth. Wild hedgehogs eat insects, worms, slugs, millipedes, frogs, lizards, mice, and even poisonous snakes and fruit. They feed mainly at night.

Some hedgehogs make their homes in people's gardens. They will drink milk from a saucer.

Where do Hedgehogs Live ?

Hedgehogs do not live in all parts of the world. The kind of hedgehog in the story lives in Europe. Other kinds of hedgehog live in Africa and in Asia. But there are no hedgehogs in America or Australia. The porcupine which lives in America has

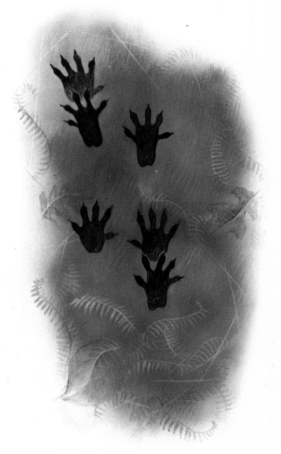

A hedgehog's footprints

quills which look like big spines, but it is not related to the hedgehogs at all.

Is It True ?

Many stories have been told about hedgehogs and nobody knows whether they are true or not. Some people laugh at farmers for believing that hedgehogs steal milk from cows. But other people say that they have seen them sucking milk from them.

Some people also think that hedgehogs steal apples and strawberries. The picture below was drawn long, long ago. It shows some hedgehogs rolling on their backs under some trees. Their spines have stuck into the fallen fruit. Not many people have ever seen a hedgehog doing this. But many people believe that they do.

Foam Bath

Hedgehogs have another strange habit. They lick things with their tongues until foam comes out of their mouths. Then they stand on their front legs and twist their heads around to smear the foam on their spines. Sometimes they turn so hard that they fall right over. Scientists cannot think why they do this. But maybe one day they will find out.

An old picture of hedgehogs stealing fruit

ACC # 1624

599
SHE
    Sheehan, Angela
      The hedgehog

DATE DUE

ACC # 1624

599
SHE
    Sheehan, Angela
      The hedgehog

DATE DUE	BORROWER'S NAME
	ORlaNdo HARRis
4-8	Reva Wilson 12
4-1	Willis S. Salmon R/2